flower**power**

flower**power**

cooking with petals, blossoms and blooms

author **Kathy Brown** photographer **Michelle Garrett**

LORENZ BOOKS

First published in 2000 by Lorenz Books

© Anness Publishing Limited 2000

Lorenz Books is an imprint of Anness Publishing Limited,
Hermes House, 88–89 Blackfriars Road, London SE1 8HA

Published in the USA by Lorenz Books, Anness Publishing Inc.,
27 West 20th Street, New York, NY 10011; (800) 354 9657

A CIP catalogue record for this book is available from
the British Library

Publisher Joanna Lorenz
Editor Sarah Ainley
Project editor Molly Perham
Designer Jane Coney
Jacket design Wilson Harvey
Photography Michelle Garrett
Food for photography Joanna Farrow
Indexer Helen Snaith
Editorial reader Kate Sillence

10 9 8 7 6 5 4 3 2 1

contents

introduction

Flowers have been used for culinary purposes for centuries, either pickled or candied, made into syrup, used on salads, or transformed into wines or cordials. Modern ways of cooking are not nearly as elaborate or time-consuming as the methods employed in previous decades and centuries, and many of the edible ideas given here are instant in their results, using flowers as beautiful garnishes or tasty additions. Such ideas suit modern lifestyles, which require the quick and easy approach. Yet these are quite simply some of the best ways of cooking with flowers, keeping them fresh, fragrant and flavoursome at the same time.

Visual attractiveness or "eye appeal" is one of the most important aspects of preparing food. A few fresh borage flowers will give a whole new look to a summer fruit platter. A sprinkling of daisy petals makes a beautiful carefree topping for a fruit dessert, and a handful of nasturtium flowers scattered over a salad of garden leaves will completely transform it, not only in appearance, but in texture and flavour as well. Sugared petals and fresh flowers preserved in butter make charming details for the tea table, while cordials, tisanes and punches flavoured and decorated with wild flowers from fields and hedgerows evoke the traditions of time gone by.

Some of the recipes in this book will involve a little more time in the kitchen, but they are certainly worth it. The floral ice bowl and the rose-petal sorbet, for example, are both made over a matter of hours, but I think you will agree, the results are spectacular. Floral oils may sound complicated, but actually take very little time at all. Crystallizing petals takes a little longer perhaps, but with a paintbrush in hand, the whole exercise can be therapeutic and the results taste delicious.

As well as the specific recipes, I am sure you will find a good use for the Plant Directory at the back of the book, which gives you all the information you need on how best to use a particular edible flower in the kitchen.

I hope that by showing you how to use edible flowers in new ways, this book will succeed in opening your eyes and imagination to a wealth of interesting new scents, sights, textures and tastes.

KATHY BROWN

edible flowers in history

The Romans used mallows, alpine pinks, violets and roses in their dishes, as well as lavender in sauces, but they were by no means the first. Pot marigolds and orange blossom have been used for over a thousand years in Eastern cookery, while lilies and chrysanthemums have been used for even longer.

In the 16th century, Europe experienced an unprecedented interest in gardening and garden design, and much was learnt about growing, using and conserving flowers in the home. With the exploration of new lands, foreign plants were introduced to Europe, resulting in a great cross-fertilization of knowledge between the New and Old Worlds. These were exciting times, and fortunately much has been recorded.

In England at this time the Tudor still-room was a major force in the art of using herbs and flowers throughout the home, and the practice reached new heights of ornamentation in the 17th-century Stuart era. But in the years between this heyday and the middle of the 19th century, the skills were largely forgotten.

When Eleanour Sinclair Rohde (1881–1950) wrote *A Garden of Herbs* in 1920, it was to instruct readers about growing and using herbs as had been done in the past. Through her detailed research we are able to glimpse into the kitchens and still-rooms of bygone times, such treasure troves of scents and flavours.

In the kitchen a stove would be kept burning to keep the air warm and dry, just right for drying and storing the herbs and flowers needed for the household. In houses great and small, the pantry would be stocked with bottles of rose water and rose oil, and glass jars would contain vinegars flavoured with marjoram, cowslips, violets, clove-scented alpine pinks and carnations. There would be jars of floral conserves, jellies and syrups, as well as boxes of candied flowers, sugared pastes, and many other treats besides.

candied flowers

The art of preserving flowers in sugar has been a favourite since records began. Petals and whole flowers would be individually sugared, or they would be made into "drops" or "sugar paste", to be cut and eaten in much the same way as candies today.

William Rabisha recorded in *The Whole Body of Cookery Dissected* (1675) how "To Candy Rose Leaves as Natural as if They Grow on Trees." He recommended spreading red or damask rose petals on paper, and sprinkling them with rose water and sugar. The petals are left in the sunshine, and should be sprinkled with rose water and sugar several times before they have dried and candied.

floral drinks

Another popular way to use flowers was as a flavouring for drinks such as cordials, wines, liqueurs and brandy. This 18th-century recipe for adding fragrant orange flowers to brandy comes from E. Smith's *The Compleat Housewife* (1736): "Take a gallon of French brandy, boil a pound of orange flowers a little while, and put them in, save the water and with that make a syrup to sweeten it."

floral salads

One of the most exciting ways that flowers were used for the table was as a "strewing" flower on salads. In the 17th century, salads were greatly esteemed and many recipes have been recorded in minute detail. King James II's head gardener thought there should be at least 35 ingredients in an ordinary salad.

Roots would be used, such as elecampagne, daisy, fennel, angelica, rampion, parsnip and carrot; these were candied, blanched, or boiled, and added when cold or pickled. The greenery was made up of sowthistle leaves, young spinach, young primrose and violet leaves, tarragon ▶

and rocket (arugula), hyssop sage, thyme, pot marigold and marjoram, lettuce, mallow leaves, purslane, cowslip, cress, young basil, borage and bugloss leaves, chervil, samphire, plantain and yarrow, vine tendrils and wood sorrel.

Salads could be grand affairs, often the centre of a banquet, and flowers would be an integral part of them. Favourite spring and summer flowers included borage, violet, rosemary, primrose, nasturtium and pot marigold: the "strewing" of these flowers must have been a wonderful sight. In the middle of winter fresh flowers were not available so salads were presented with flowers preserved in vinegar or candied in sugar, with savoury pickles and sweet candied flowers sitting side by side. The winter array was quite different in taste and texture, but what a rich variety of flavours our ancestors still managed to enjoy.

popular flowers
in the past

Flowers were very much a part of kitchen life in the 16th and 17th centuries, and violets, roses, rosemary, gillyflower, lavender and cowslips were among the most popular. It is fascinating to see just how many recipes were available for any one of these flowers, but cowslips particularly so.

Cowslips grew in grasslands and meadows, and were picked in springtime to be strewn in salads, pickled for winter, made into syrups, candied or creamed. One of the best-loved treats was cowslip wine, which was popular until the 20th century and was mentioned by Mrs Beeton in her *Household Management*, first published in 1861. Cowslip mead was also popular, using honey, sweet briar and lemon for flavouring. Other wine recipes of the 16th and 17th centuries included primrose, broom, mint, clover, meadowsweet, fennel, hawthorn blossom and tansy but these had all but disappeared from mainstream cookery books by the end of the 19th century.

Plenty of fruit and herb recipes have survived since the last century, but not recipes for edible flowers, and it has taken almost 100 years to revive and reshape the old ideas for using flowers at the dining tables of today.

gathering
flowers

Ideally, flowers should be gathered on a warm dry morning, before the sun has become too strong and drawn out the essential oils. They are best picked in bud or freshly opened, when their scent and flavour are at their most enticing. When picking flowers for culinary purposes, they should be organically home-grown: plants from nurseries or garden centres may have been treated with pesticides. Ignore dusty or dirty flowers from roadsides and avoid any that may have been sprayed with insecticide.

Those who are allergic to pollen should not eat flowers. In any case, it is still best to cut out the central reproductive areas, where the stamens and pollen are to be found, if you can. Individual flowers vary a great deal but some, such as lilies, hibiscus and hollyhocks, are very heavy with pollen and it is easy to see the parts to be removed. With smaller flowers such as primroses, violets, cowslips, violas, sage, chives, marjoram and basil it is more difficult, so if anyone is susceptible to allergy it is best to avoid all flowers.

WARNING

This book lists flowers which are commonly edible (*see* Plant Directory). However, the list is not exhaustive. Meanwhile, there are plenty of flowers around the world which are most definitely not safe to eat, such as euphorbia, rhododendron, anemone, aquilegia, helleborus, hedera, wisteria and laburnum, to name but a few. If in any doubt at all, do NOT eat them. Stick to those listed in the Plant Directory where there are plenty of glorious, pretty and tasty flowers which are safe to use and are perfectly delicious. Moreover, they have been tried and tested for generations.

the versatile rose

Throughout history, the rose has been used in a wide range of sweet recipes. Rose water, rose-flavoured honey, rose oil, rose candies, rose sugar, rose-petal jam, rose-petal jelly and rose butter are just some of its uses. Crystallized roses, either petals or whole flowers, make cakes and desserts really special.

In order to make successful preparations in the kitchen with rose petals, it is essential to use the sweetly scented varieties. There are a great many to choose from, including nearly all the old-fashioned roses with their full petals and sweet perfume, such as the pink-and-white striped 'Rosa Mundi'; moss roses, including 'William Lobb' with its magenta pink flowers; and Bourbon roses, such as the pink 'Louise Odier' and the deeper pink 'Mme Isaac Pereire', both of which flower from mid-summer to mid-autumn. The climber 'Cecile Brunner' is exceptional for its pale pink, scroll-like buds, which are perfect for crystallizing whole. Other climbers, such as dark red 'Guinée' and pink 'Zéphirine Drouhin', are recommended as well.

Many of David Austin's breed of English roses are highly scented, including pink 'Mary Rose', apricot 'Evelyn', deep purple 'The Prince' and rich pink, gloriously scented 'Gertrude Jekyll'. Neat little 'Cambridgeshire' is a vibrant mix of pinky-red and yellow and looks lovely scattered over a bowl of fresh strawberries. These are just a few favourites, but there are scores of others besides.

rose-petal and strawberry punch

This makes a memorable party piece with its colourful petals and deep pink colour. Use raspberries instead of strawberries if you prefer.

Serves 8–10

1 BOTTLE OF ROSÉ WINE, CHILLED

60ML/4TBSP VODKA

75G/3OZ STRAWBERRIES, SLICED

HANDFUL OF SCENTED ROSE PETALS, WHITE HEELS AT THE
  BASE REMOVED

1 BOTTLE OF CARBONATED MINERAL WATER

1 Pour the chilled bottle of rosé wine into a glass punch bowl. Add the vodka and the sliced strawberries.

2 Scatter a handful of scented rose petals on top. Chill the punch in the refrigerator for about 1 hour, and pour in the bottle of carbonated mineral water just before serving.

iced rose-petal cake

An iced sponge cake, filled with a layer of sweet-tasting rose-petal butter and adorned with crystallized roses, is a delightful way to mark a summer celebration.

Serves 10–12

FOR THE CAKE

225G/8OZ BUTTER OR
    MARGARINE, SOFTENED
225G/8OZ CASTER
    (SUPERFINE) SUGAR
4 MEDIUM EGGS
225G/8OZ SELF-RAISING
    FLOUR
5ML/1 TSP BAKING POWDER

FOR THE FILLING

1 QUANTITY ROSE-PETAL
    BUTTER (SEE BELOW)

TO DECORATE

225G/8OZ ICING
    (CONFECTIONER'S) SUGAR
30ML/2TBSP ROSE WATER
6–8 PINK ROSES, AND
    SEVERAL ROSE PETALS,
    CRYSTALLIZED

1 Preheat the oven to 180°C/350°F/Gas 4. Grease two 20cm/8in round sandwich tins. Put the cake ingredients in a large bowl and beat until light and creamy. Divide between the tins and bake for 25 minutes, or until firm.

2 Cool on a wire rack, then sandwich the cake together on a serving plate with the rose-petal butter mix.

3 Beat the icing (confectioner's) sugar in a bowl with rose water to give a consistency that thickly coats the back of a spoon. Spoon the icing over the cake. Decorate with a circle of crystallized roses and petals.

rose-petal butter

This recipe combines scented rose petals with butter and icing sugar to create a sweet cake filling. Any leftover mixture can be covered with cling film (plastic wrap) and kept in the fridge for up to 2 weeks.

Makes enough to fill a 20cm/8in cake

60ML/4TBSP SWEETLY SCENTED PETALS
115G/4OZ BUTTER, SOFTENED
115G/4OZ ICING SUGAR

1 Remove the white heels from the base of the rose petals. Beat the butter in a bowl until it is creamy in colour. Stir in the icing sugar, a little at a time, and add the rose petals.

2 Spread between two halves of a sponge cake, or use as butter icing (frosting) in fairy (cup) cakes.

rose-petal sorbet

This sorbet with its fabulous flavour of roses makes a wonderful end to a summer meal. Use the most scented variety you can find in the garden. Pick fresh blooms that are newly opened, ideally in the late morning, before the heat of the day evaporates the essential oils.

Serves 4–6

115G/4OZ CASTER
(SUPERFINE) SUGAR
300ML/½PT/1¼ CUPS
BOILING WATER
PETALS OF 3 LARGE,
SCENTED ROSES

JUICE OF 2 LEMONS
300ML/½PT/1¼ CUPS
ROSÉ WINE
TO DECORATE
WHOLE CRYSTALLIZED
ROSES OR ROSE PETALS

1 Stir the sugar into the water in a bowl until it has dissolved. Remove the white heels at the base of the petals, then add to the bowl. Leave to cool.

2 Blend the mixture in a food processor, then strain. Add the lemon juice and wine and pour into a freezer container. Freeze until the mixture has frozen around the edges.

3 Turn the sorbet into a mixing bowl and whisk until smooth. Re-freeze it until frozen around the edges. Repeat the whisking and freezing process once or twice more, until the sorbet is pale and smooth. Freeze until firm.

4 Serve the sorbet decorated with crystallized roses or rose petals.

floral ice bowl

This is a dramatic way to show off some of the most beautiful edible flowers. Use the ice bowl to serve ice creams and sorbets, chilled frosted fruit or other cold desserts. When the dessert has been served, the ice will slowly melt and the flowers will look even more ephemeral and beautiful.

Makes 1 large bowl

A SELECTION OF PINK ROSES, BUDS AND LEAVES

12 SMALL FLOWERS, SUCH AS VIOLAS, SMALL ALPINE
  PINKS OR DAISIES

ICE CUBES

1 Scatter several roses, buds, small flowers and sprigs of leaves into the base of a 3.1l/5½pt bowl. Make sure that the flowers do not touch each other. Weigh them down with plenty of ice cubes.

2 Rest a 1.7l/3pt bowl over the ice so that it sits in the centre. Pour cold water between the bowls until the water comes about 4cm/1½in up the sides. If the smaller bowl starts to move, tuck crumpled paper towels between the bowls so it remains in the centre. Put in the freezer and place weights in the centre.

3 Remove from the freezer and discard the weights. Tuck more flowers, petals and leaves between the bowls and top up to 5mm/¼in of the rim with water. Freeze for at least 5 hours until solid. Remove from the freezer and leave for 5 minutes.

4 Fill a washing up bowl with hot water and immerse the bowls for a few seconds. Invert them on to a plate and lift away the outer bowl. To remove the centre bowl, turn it the right way up, pour some hot water into the centre and twist the bowl until it will lift out.

seasonal salads

Many flowers make wonderful additions to salads and yet few are used on a day-to-day basis. We may be familiar with nasturtiums and chives, but how many of us have used the crunchy mangetout (snow pea) flavour of day lilies or the punchy, nutty flavour of sweet rocket flowers to pep up a salad?

There are many qualities inherent in salad flowers. First, there is texture: some, such as hollyhocks and evening primroses, are silky smooth to eat; others, such as day lilies and chives, have a definite crunchy quality. Second, there is flavour: sweet cicely and fennel taste of aniseed; nasturtiums are hot and peppery; while salad rocket (arugula) is nutty. Borage tastes just like cucumber, while sage, thyme and marjoram flowers taste like a sweeter version of the leaves. The same is true of rosemary, basil and hyssop.

Then there is colour. Pot marigolds are available in vibrant oranges and yellows. Nasturtiums and sunflowers are equally vibrant, and also come in shades of red. Day lilies grow in different shades – the attractive orange is the most common. Anchusa is a brilliant blue; hyssop and sage are almost as strong. Borage is a softer blue but particularly striking with its central area of black stamens. Bergamot might be pink or red, while hollyhocks range from almost black to the palest yellow or white. Primroses, cowslips, fennel and dill will provide yellow – but the best yellow of all is evening primrose.

salad flowers
through the seasons

In springtime, pale yellow primroses make a tasty and pretty salad ingredient, as do both purple and white scented violets. Use the flowers sprinkled over hard-boiled eggs, cucumber, tomatoes or a bed of lettuce. Slightly later, sweet-smelling cowslips and colourful pink, red or white double daisies can be used to equally good effect. Rosemary flowers are small, but sweet and tasty, and a beautiful blue.

In late spring and early summer sweet cicely is in flower. Its tiny lacy white blooms have a strong aniseed flavour that will add a distinctive taste to the simplest salad. The leaves and, later, the semi-ripe seeds have the same flavour. Chives also come into flower – their lilac domes of pungent, onion-flavoured florets make a pretty, crunchy addition to eggs or lettuce. Soon sage is in bloom, with a succession of tasty tubular flowers, and pot marigolds with their colourful petals. Borage is a favourite flower at this time of year – the exquisite combination of black and blue colouring, delicate shape and sweet cucumber flavour is superb. Anchusa may not be high on flavour, but its intense blue is wonderful set against a simple orange salad.

By early summer scented alpine pinks, scented geraniums and sweet rocket (arugula) are in flower, and tall hollyhocks and papery hibiscus unfurl their exquisite blooms. The graceful, tubular flowers of pineapple sage are sweet and delicious, and are quite spectacular in their brilliant red vestments. All these flowers will grace a summer fruit salad bowl, and may equally well be used in green salads.

Later in the season, flowers such as pink or red bergamot, fiery coloured nasturtiums and sunflowers are excellent in leafy salads. Young bergamot and nasturtium leaves can be added for texture, shape and flavour. Slices of dark beetroot (beets) look wonderful decorated with such vibrant colours. Yellow flowers of dill and fennel are always good with a salad, or with fish or pâté. Basil flowers are small, but they taste deliciously sweet and will transform a simple tomato salad. Thyme and hyssop flowers are also small, but they are colourful and tasty and should be used quite freely, especially with chicken. Marjorams or oreganos have a warm, aromatic quality to the flowers that makes them a valuable addition to a pizza or salad. All the mints will flower, so use them to add interest to almost any green salad. Mint flowers will also make a wonderful salad vinaigrette.

violet and primrose salad

Violet and primrose flowers will add flavour and colour to any spring salad. Simply mix your favourite ingredients and arrange the flowers on top. Pick the freshest blooms, place the stems in water and use the same day.

Serves 4

2 SPRING ONIONS (SCALLIONS)

2 RIPE AVOCADOS

30ML/2TBSP LEMON JUICE

150G/5OZ MILD GOAT'S
   CHEESE

SMALL HANDFUL EACH OF
   PRIMROSES AND VIOLETS

FOR THE DRESSING

90ML/6TBSP LIGHT OLIVE OIL

30ML/2TBSP WHITE WINE
   VINEGAR

5ML/1TSP DRY MUSTARD

5ML/1TSP CASTER
   (SUPERFINE) SUGAR

SALT AND FRESHLY GROUND
   BLACK PEPPER

1 To make the dressing, use a fork to mix together all the ingredients in a bowl. Chill in the fridge until required.

2 Trim the spring onions (scallions). Cut lengthways into thin shreds, then across into 5cm/2in lengths. Put in a bowl of cold water so that the shreds curl. Leave in a cool place for an hour.

3 Halve and stone (pit) the avocados and peel away the skins. Slice very finely and toss in a bowl with lemon juice to prevent discoloration. Cut the cheese into small pieces. Remove all the green parts from the primroses and violets.

4 To serve, scatter the avocado and cheese on to serving plates and add the drained spring onions. Finish with the primrose and violet flowers and spoon over the dressing.

anchusa, orange and watercress salad

Anchusa flowers make a delightful decoration on a sliced orange salad. The colours make the dish vibrant and fresh, especially set against the deep green of the watercress, with the dark stain of balsamic vinegar cast over the oranges.

Serves 4

12 ANCHUSA FLOWERS

2 SEEDLESS ORANGES

1 BUNCH WATERCRESS

FOR THE DRESSING

15ML/1TBSP BALSAMIC
VINEGAR

60ML/4TBSP OLIVE OIL

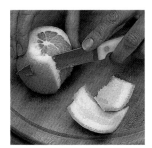

1 To prepare the flowers for the salad, remove the flower-head from the green calyx by gently teasing it out.

2 Peel the oranges and slice horizontally into thin sections. Arrange on a salad plate, surrounded by sprigs of watercress.

3 Scatter the anchusa flowers over the oranges, then drizzle with a mixture of balsamic vinegar and olive oil. Eat with cold duck or pâté and plenty of French bread.

early summer salad with *sage and chive* flowers

The flavours of sage and chives complement each other perfectly in this tasty salad.

Serves 4–6

2 LITTLE GEM LETTUCES

100G/3½OZ SUGAR SNAP
  PEAS

¼ CUCUMBER

2 STICKS CELERY

HANDFUL EACH OF SAGE
  AND CHIVE FLOWERS

FOR THE DRESSING

60ML/4TBSP MILD OLIVE OIL

10ML/2TSP LEMON JUICE

COARSE SALT AND FRESHLY
  GROUND BLACK PEPPER

1 Separate the lettuce leaves and tear larger ones into smaller pieces. Halve the sugar snap peas lengthways. Halve and thinly slice the cucumber. Slice the celery diagonally. Toss the salad ingredients in a bowl with the sage and chive flowers.

2 Mix the olive oil with the lemon juice and seasoning and spoon over the salad. Toss lightly.

late summer salad
with nasturtiums

The mild, peppery taste of nasturtiums makes them excellent for salads. Choose the freshest blooms, and eat whole or just use the petals. The leaves, buds and seeds can also be eaten.

Serves 4–6

ABOUT 16 YOUNG
   NASTURTIUM LEAVES
MIXED SALAD LEAVES
2–3 BOILED BEETROOT
   (BEETS)
ABOUT 16 WHOLE
   NASTURTIUM FLOWERS,
   STEMS REMOVED
ABOUT 4–6 NASTURTIUM
   FLOWER BUDS

FOR THE DRESSING
4 CRUSHED NASTURTIUM
   SEEDS
60ML/4TBSP WALNUT OR
   OLIVE OIL
10ML/2TSP WHITE WINE OR
   BALSAMIC VINEGAR
COARSE SALT AND FRESHLY
   GROUND BLACK PEPPER

1 Create an outer wall of young nasturtium leaves around the edge of a deep salad bowl. Add an inner wall of mixed green salad leaves.

2 Slice the beetroot (beets) thinly and place in layers between the salad leaves.

3 Decorate the salad leaves with the nasturtium flowers and buds, leaving one whole flower for the centre.

4 Mix together the dressing ingredients in a small bowl. Toss the salad in the dressing just before serving.

hollyhock and nectarine salad

The fresh, juicy flavour and beautiful colouring of nectarines lend themselves to an arrangement with hollyhock petals. Choose hollyhock petals to contrast or blend with the fruit.

Serves 2

2 NECTARINES, EITHER WHITE OR YELLOW FLESH

2 HOLLYHOCK FLOWERS

2 SPRIGS FLOWERING GINGER MINT

1 Cut the nectarines in half, remove the stones (pits) and slice the fruit. Arrange the slices on individual serving plates.

3 Arrange the petals around the nectarine slices and garnish with the mint flowers.

2 Remove the stigma from the centre of each hollyhock. Cut off all the green parts so that you have five petals. Brush any excess pollen off the petals.

summer fruit platter
with borage flowers

Summer berries look sumptuous topped with bright blue borage flowers. This idea can be kept simple, using just two types of fruit, or wonderfully luxurious as seen here.

Serves 6–8

3–4 PASSION FRUIT

HALF A MELON

350G/12OZ STRAWBERRIES

115G/4OZ CHERRIES

100G/3½OZ BLUEBERRIES

115G/4OZ RASPBERRIES

12–15 BORAGE FLOWERS

FOR THE PUREE

225G/8OZ RASPBERRIES

15ML/1TBSP ICING
 (CONFECTIONER'S) SUGAR

TO SERVE

CASTER (SUPERFINE) SUGAR
 AND WHIPPED CREAM

1 Prepare the fruit. Cut the passion fruit in half. Make melon balls if you have a melon baller, otherwise cut into chunks. Slice a few strawberries in half, leaving the rest whole with their green calyx intact. The cherries can be left with their stalks. The blueberries and raspberries should be left whole.

3 Arrange the fruit on a large serving plate, leaving the middle of the plate clear. Spoon the raspberry purée down the centre of the platter, through the berries and melon. Chill until ready to serve.

4 Just before serving, arrange the borage flowers over the purée. Offer caster (superfine) sugar and softly whipped cream at the table.

2 For the purée, press the raspberries through a sieve into a bowl to extract the seeds. Stir in the icing (confectioner's) sugar, adding a little more if necessary to sweeten.

savoury delights

The strongly aromatic flavours of herbs such as basil, marjoram, thyme and lavender are a wonderful complement to savoury food. Both flowers and leaves can be used fresh in all sorts of ways to flavour soups, salads, quiches, pastas and stuffings, as well as egg, chicken and fish dishes.

ciabatta bread with marjoram flowers

Here is a simple but tasty recipe using marjoram flowers. Extras such as capers, olives, anchovies or (bell) peppers can also be added.

Serves 2

1 CIABATTA LOAF
4 MEDIUM TOMATOES
115G/4OZ MOZZARELLA OR
   CHEDDAR CHEESE,
   SLICED OR GRATED
15ML/1TBSP OLIVE OIL
SALT AND FRESHLY GROUND
   BLACK PEPPER
15ML/1TBSP MARJORAM
   FLOWERS

1 Cut the loaf in half lengthways and toast under the grill (broiler).

2 Slash the skin of the tomatoes and pour boiling water over them. Allow to cool, remove the skin and cut into slices.

3 Lightly drizzle oil over the bread and cover with the cheese and tomato slices. Season and scatter over the marjoram flowers. Drizzle with a little more olive oil. Return to the grill until the cheese melts.

chilled tomato and basil-flower soup

This is a really fresh tasting soup, packed with the complementary flavours of tomato and basil and topped with sweet basil flowers.

Serves 4

900G/2LB TOMATOES

1 ONION

1 CLOVE GARLIC, CRUSHED

15ML/1TBSP OLIVE OIL

600ML/1PT/2½ CUPS
   VEGETABLE STOCK

20 BASIL LEAVES

A FEW DROPS OF ELDER-
   FLOWER OR BALSAMIC
   VINEGAR

JUICE OF ½ LEMON

150ML/¼PT/⅔ CUP PLAIN
   YOGURT

SUGAR AND SALT, TO TASTE

TO GARNISH

30ML/2TBSP PLAIN
   YOGURT

8 SMALL BASIL LEAVES

10ML/2TSP BASIL FLOWERS,
   GREEN PARTS REMOVED

1 Chop the tomatoes roughly, then peel and chop the onion and garlic. Fry the onion and garlic in the oil for 2–3 minutes.

2 Add 300ml/½pt/ 1¼ cups vegetable stock to the pan, then add the tomatoes. Bring to the boil, lower the heat and simmer for 15 minutes.

3 Allow to cool slightly, liquidize and sieve to remove the tomato skins and seeds.

4 Add the remainder of the stock, half the basil leaves, vinegar, lemon juice and yogurt. Season with sugar and salt to taste. Process until smooth. Chill.

5 Just before serving finely shred the remaining basil leaves and add to the soup. Pour the chilled soup into individual bowls.

6 Garnish with yogurt topped with a few small basil leaves and a scattering of basil flowers on each serving.

roasted peppers
with sweet cicely

This is a dish full of flavour with a beautiful, intense colour to match. The red (bell) peppers are cooked with tomatoes and scattered with semi-ripe sweet cicely seeds, fennel seeds and capers, with sweet cicely flowers added on top. The whole dish is then roasted with olive oil.

Serves 4

8 SMALL OR 4 MEDIUM
   TOMATOES
4 RED (BELL) PEPPERS,
   HALVED AND DESEEDED
15ML/1TBSP SEMI-RIPE
   SWEET CICELY SEEDS
15ML/1TBSP FENNEL SEEDS
15ML/1TBSP CAPERS
8 SWEET CICELY FLOWERS,
   NEWLY OPENED
60ML/4TBSP OLIVE OIL
TO GARNISH
A FEW SMALL SWEET
   CICELY LEAVES
8 MORE FLOWERS, NEWLY
   OPENED, STEMS REMOVED

1 To skin the tomatoes, cut a cross at the base, then pour over boiling water and leave to stand for 5 minutes. Cut the tomatoes in half if they are of medium size.

2 Place the (bell) pepper halves in an ovenproof dish. Fill with tomatoes. Preheat the oven to 180°C/350°F/Gas 4.

3 Scatter the sweet cicely seeds, fennel seeds and capers and about half the sweet cicely flowers on top. Drizzle the olive oil all over. Bake in the oven for 1 hour.

4 Remove from the oven and add the rest of the flowers. Garnish with sweet cicely flowers and leaves – the leaves taste just like the flowers and make an excellent garnish.

provençal thyme mushrooms

Here, fresh thyme flowers have been added to roasted mushrooms topped with breadcrumbs. The result is a wonderfully aromatic taste of the Mediterranean.

Serves 8

8 LARGE MUSHROOMS
120ML/8TBSP WHITE BREADCRUMBS
30ML/2TBSP THYME LEAVES
2 CLOVES GARLIC
45ML/3TBSP OLIVE OIL
30ML/2TBSP THYME FLOWERS
COARSE SALT AND FRESHLY GROUND BLACK PEPPER

1 Clean and skin the mushrooms. Remove and chop the stalks. Place the mushrooms cup side up on a large ovenproof dish.

2 Blend the bread, mushroom stalks, thyme leaves and garlic in a food processor. Add plenty of salt and pepper, and 15ml/1tbsp olive oil. Then mix in 15ml/1tbsp thyme flowers.

3 Preheat the oven to 230°C/450°F/Gas 8. Divide the bread mixture between the mushrooms and drizzle over the remaining olive oil.

4 Cook in the hot oven until the mushrooms are soft and the breadcrumbs lightly browned. Scatter over the remaining flowers just before serving.

scrambled eggs with chive flowers

Scrambled eggs on toast is one of the simplest and quickest meals, taking only a matter of minutes to prepare and cook. By adding finely chopped parsley and chive leaves and a handful of lilac-pink chive flowers, it is transformed into something much more tasty and certainly far more imaginative.

Serves 2

30ML/2TBSP CHIVE FLOWERS, PLUS EXTRA TO GARNISH (PICK THE FRESHEST FLOWERS)

30ML/2TBSP CHOPPED CHIVE LEAVES (PICK YOUNG LEAVES)

15ML/1TBSP CHOPPED PARSLEY (PICK THE FRESHEST LEAVES)

4 EGGS

60ML/4TBSP MILK OR CREAM

50G/2OZ BUTTER

SALT AND FRESHLY GROUND BLACK PEPPER

TO SERVE

4 SLICES OF BUTTERED TOAST

1 Cut the chive flower-heads from the main stem, then snip off each floret, removing as much of the stems as possible.

2 Chop the chive and parsley finely and mix with the chive flowers.

3 Beat the eggs and seasoning with the milk or cream.

4 Melt the butter and pour in the egg mixture and cook over a low heat. Stir for a minute or two until the mixture is just beginning to thicken.

5 Add the chive leaves and flowers and the parsley. Serve the eggs with hot buttered toast with extra chive flowers, to garnish.

nasturtium omelette

Nasturtium flowers are full of colour and have a mild, peppery taste that is good in omelettes. This is a spectacularly quick and easy way to serve nasturtium flowers.

Serves 1

50G/2OZ YOUNG TENDER
   RUNNER BEANS

2 EGGS

30ML/2TBSP MILK

2 NASTURTIUM SEEDS

2 YOUNG NASTURTIUM
   LEAVES

4 NASTURTIUMS, PETALS
   ONLY

15ML/1TBSP BUTTER

FRESHLY GRATED
   PARMESAN CHEESE,
   TO TASTE

SALT AND FRESHLY GROUND
   BLACK PEPPER

TO GARNISH

NASTURTIUM PETALS

1 Slice the runner beans very finely. Add them to a saucepan of boiling water and boil for about 4 minutes. Drain well.

2 In a bowl, beat the eggs with the milk.

3 Crush the nasturtium seeds with a fork. Add the seeds, leaves and petals to the beaten egg mixture in the bowl. Season well with salt and freshly ground black pepper.

4 Melt the butter in a frying pan. Pour the egg and nasturtium mixture into the pan, add the beans and cook gently until the omelette has set.

5 Sprinkle the omelette with freshly grated Parmesan cheese and serve immediately, garnished with extra nasturtium petals.

bergamot rice salad

The beautiful red bergamot flowers are a striking contrast to the glistening black olives, mushrooms and wild rice. Serve with fresh mackerel or white fish.

Serves 4–6

250G/8OZ WILD RICE OR
MIXED RICE WITH WILD
RICE GRAINS

225G/8OZ FLAT MUSHROOMS,
THICKLY SLICED
30ML/2TBSP OLIVE OIL
4 YOUNG BERGAMOT
LEAVES, THINLY SHREDDED
115G/4OZ BLACK OLIVES
15–30ML/1–2TBSP OF PINK
OR RED BERGAMOT PETALS
SALT AND FRESHLY GROUND
BLACK PEPPER

1 Simmer the rice in a pan of boiling water for 25–30 minutes until soft, then drain.

2 Place the sliced mushrooms in a frying pan with the olive oil and cook gently for 4 minutes.

3 Add the bergamot leaves and olives. Season to taste.

4 Add the cooked wild rice and toss all the ingredients together. Mix in the bergamot petals.

lavender chicken

Here, lavender flowers are used to perfume and flavour chicken cooked in a large casserole with red wine, oranges and thyme. When the lid is removed after cooking, the heady aroma will entice as much as the delicious flavour.

Serves 4

15ML/1TBSP BUTTER

15ML/1TBSP OLIVE OIL

8 CHICKEN PIECES

8 SHALLOTS

30ML/2TBSP FLOUR

250ML/8FL OZ/1 CUP RED
   WINE

250ML/8FL OZ/1 CUP
   CHICKEN STOCK

4 SPRIGS THYME

10ML/2TSP THYME FLOWERS

10ML/2TSP LAVENDER
   FLOWERS

GRATED ZEST AND JUICE
   OF 1 ORANGE

SALT AND FRESHLY GROUND
   BLACK PEPPER

TO GARNISH

1 ORANGE, DIVIDED
   INTO SEGMENTS

12 LAVENDER SPRIGS

1 Heat the butter and olive oil in a heavy-based frying pan and add the chicken pieces. Brown all over. Transfer to a large flameproof casserole.

2 Cook the shallots in the frying pan for 2 minutes, then add to the casserole.

3 Add the flour to the frying pan, stir and cook for 2 minutes. Pour in enough wine and stock to make a thin sauce, bring to the boil, stirring all the time. Season to taste. Stir in the thyme sprigs, thyme and lavender flowers, orange rind and juice.

4 Pour the sauce over the chicken. Cover the casserole and simmer for 30–40 minutes until the chicken is tender.

5 Remove the thyme sprigs from the casserole before serving. Serve the chicken garnished with the orange segments and lavender sprigs.

sweet treats

Crystallized flowers add a touch of luxury to cakes, biscuits, desserts and ice creams. Cowslips, pinks, roses, primroses and violets are particularly effective, either used whole or as petals. Fresh daisy petals, or sprays of flowers such as verbena and elderflower, can also be used to make a decorative topping.

blackcurrant mousse with daisies

Here, daisy petals add a simple, carefree topping to a blackcurrant dessert.

Serves 4–6

800G/1¾LB FRESH OR
   FROZEN BLACKCURRANTS
150G/5OZ CASTER
   (SUPERFINE) SUGAR

450ML/¾PT/SCANT 2 CUPS
   PLAIN YOGURT
TO DECORATE
SPRIGS OF BLACKCURRANTS
PINK AND RED DAISIES

1 Put the blackcurrants in a saucepan with 90ml/6 tbsp water and the sugar. Cover tightly and simmer gently for about 10 minutes until the fruit is soft and pulpy. Blend in a food processor, then press through a sieve and leave to cool.

2 Stir the yogurt into the purée until evenly combined, then spoon the mixture into serving glasses and chill until ready to serve. Add the blackcurrant sprigs to the top, then gently pull the quills from the daisies and scatter over.

rose geranium roulade

This recipe uses 'Attar of Roses' leaves to give flavour to the roulade itself, while using the colour of 'Capitatum' petals for the decoration.

Serves 6

12–16 YOUNG 'ATTAR OF ROSES' GERANIUM LEAVES

5 MEDIUM EGGS, SEPARATED

275G/10OZ CASTER (SUPERFINE) SUGAR

30ML/2TBSP ICING (CONFECTIONER'S) SUGAR, PLUS EXTRA FOR DUSTING

A FEW DROPS OF ROSE WATER

300ML/½PT/1¼ CUPS DOUBLE (HEAVY) CREAM

2 KIWI FRUIT

10–15 FRESH OR CRYSTALLIZED 'CAPITATUM' GERANIUM PETALS

1 Preheat the oven to 180°C/350°F/Gas 4. Line a 20cm x 28cm/8 x 11in baking tray with greaseproof (waxed) paper and arrange the geranium leaves all over it.

2 Beat together the egg yolks and sugar until light and fluffy. In a separate bowl, whisk the egg whites until stiff and then fold into the egg yolk and sugar mixture.

3 Pour the mixture on top of the geranium leaves. Bake in the oven for about 10 minutes until just set. Remove from the oven and leave to cool.

4 Turn the roulade out on to a clean piece of greaseproof paper dusted with icing (confectioner's) sugar. Carefully remove the geranium leaves from the roulade.

5 Add a few drops of rose water to the cream and then whip until soft peaks form. Spread over the roulade. Peel and thinly slice the kiwi fruit and distribute over the surface of the cream.

6 Roll up the roulade, holding the short edges. Dust with icing sugar and arrange the geranium petals on top.

apple snow with *lemon* verbena

The recipe uses lemon verbena leaves to impart the flavour of lemon, while the delicate flowers are used to decorate the top.

Serves 4

450G/1LB COOKING APPLES, PEELED AND CORED

50G/2OZ CASTER (SUPERFINE) SUGAR

30ML/2TBSP WATER

16 YOUNG LEMON VERBENA LEAVES

2 EGG WHITES

TO DECORATE

4 SPRAYS LEMON VERBENA FLOWERS

4–8 YOUNG LEMON VERBENA LEAVES, DUSTED WITH EGG WHITE AND SUGAR

1 Slice the apples and place in a pan with the sugar, water and lemon verbena leaves. Cover and simmer gently for 10–15 minutes. Put through a sieve to make a smooth purée, then leave to cool.

2 Whisk the egg whites until stiff and fold in the apple purée.

3 Spoon into glasses and decorate with a sprinkling of lemon verbena flowers and perhaps one or two small leaves dusted with egg white and sugar.

elderflower and strawberry jam

The heady scent of elderflowers is captured in this fragrant strawberry jam. Serve it with scones and cream on a summer's afternoon, or in the depths of winter the fragrance will evoke the balmy days of summer. Once opened, keep in the fridge and consume within a week.

Makes about 4.5kg/10lb

8 ELDERFLOWER HEADS
  WITH NEWLY OPENED
  FLOWERS

3.2KG/7LB STRAWBERRIES
JUICE OF 2 LEMONS
2.75KG/6LB SUGAR

1 Cut the elderflowers off the main stem and tie the florets in a muslin (cheesecloth) bag.

2 Hull the strawberries and then mash with the lemon juice. Put in a preserving pan with the elderflowers in muslin.

3 Simmer gently until the fruit is soft, stirring frequently to prevent the fruit sticking to the bottom of the pan. Add the sugar and stir constantly until it has completely dissolved.

4 Boil rapidly until setting point is reached. To test, put a spoonful in a saucer and leave to cool. If a wrinkle forms on the top when you push it with a finger, the jam will set.

5 Remove the bag of elderflowers and any scum. Leave to cool, stir and pour into sterilized jars. Cover and label.

cowslip syllabub

Crystallized cowslips and violas make a delightful addition to many sweet dishes. Here they are used together to add artistry to a simple syllabub.

Serves 4–6

200ML/7FL OZ MEDIUM WHITE WINE

60ML/4TBSP CASTER (SUPERFINE) SUGAR

FINELY GRATED RIND AND JUICE OF 1 ORANGE

300ML/½ PT/1¼ CUPS FRESH DOUBLE (HEAVY) CREAM

TO DECORATE

A HANDFUL EACH OF CRYSTALLIZED VIOLA AND COWSLIP
FLOWERS, STALKS AND GREEN PARTS REMOVED, AND A
HANDFUL OF FRESH MINT

1 Place the wine, sugar, orange rind and juice in a bowl and leave to stand for 2 hours or more.

2 Add the mixture to the cream a little at a time, whisking until soft peaks form.

3 Spoon a little syllabub into the base of each glass. Add a few flowers, facing outwards so that they show through.

4 Add more syllabub to each glass, creating a peak in the centre of each.

5 Chill before serving. Decorate with a scattering of the violas, cowslips and mint.

meringues with crystallized pinks

One of the easiest ways to use pinks is to crystallize a few of the flowers and then add them to meringues, cakes or ice creams. You could try substituting rose- or alpine pink-flavoured sugar, instead of ordinary sugar in the meringues.

Makes about 14

4 EGG WHITES

225G/8OZ ICING (CONFEC-
TIONER'S) SUGAR (OR
LAVENDER OR ALPINE
PINK SUGAR)

10ML/2TSP VANILLA
ESSENCE (IF USING PLAIN
ICING SUGAR)

FOR THE FILLING

300ML/½PT/1¼ CUPS
DOUBLE (HEAVY) CREAM,
WHIPPED

TO DECORATE

40–50 CRYSTALLIZED
ALPINE PINK PETALS,
WHITE HEEL REMOVED
(THESE SHOULD BE MADE
ONE OR TWO DAYS
BEFORE SERVING THEM)

1 Preheat the oven to 120°C/250°F/Gas ½. Line two baking sheets with baking parchment. Whisk the egg whites until stiff. Add the sugar slowly until the mixture is glossy. Stir in the vanilla, if using.

2 Place spoonfuls of the meringue mixture on the baking sheets. Shape into nests with the back of a teaspoon.

3 Bake for 1–1¼ hours, or until the meringues are crisp. Leave to cool on a wire rack.

4 Spoon the cream into the nests and scatter the crystallized petals just before serving.

flower drinks

Flower teas, or tisanes, offer a quick, cheap and easy way of enjoying a refreshing drink, either hot or cold. Many other cold drinks, both alcoholic and non-alcoholic, are also flavoured with flowers – sparkling elderflower is one of the best known. Flowers also add flavour to a summer punch.

Many flowers are suitable for tisanes. Take a small quantity of clean flowers (in some cases, add a few leaves as well) and add a cup of boiling water. Allow to infuse for about 4 minutes, then remove the flowers and any foliage. Drink warm or chilled, and sweetened with honey if you prefer. Many flowers here can be dried and used on a later occasion. Dry them in the shade and keep them in labelled airtight tins.

Herbal teas have been used for medicinal purposes for centuries. Lavender, hyssop, thyme and marjoram were traditionally taken to alleviate cold symptoms; chamomile, hops and lime flower were recommended for insomnia. The very scent of some tisanes can act as a tonic.

Recipes still exist for drinks that few of us drink nowadays. Flowers from the fields and hedgerows, such as primrose, cowslip, clary sage, clover, meadowsweet, broom and gorse, were harvested to make wine. Chamomile and lime blossoms were used for tea and wine. Cordials and liqueurs were flavoured with violet, hawthorn and angelica. Dandelions and hops were brewed into wine and beer, while hops and cowslips were mixed with honey to make mead.

teas and
tisanes

hyssop

Put one sprig of flowering hyssop in a cup and add boiling water. Remove the flower after 4 minutes, to enjoy a beautiful pale aquamarine tisane. Drink hot or cold. It is thought to be helpful in alleviating the symptoms of colds and sore throats.

hibiscus and rosemary

Hibiscus flowers look very flamboyant but the flavour can be disappointing, so combine with a sprig of rosemary. Add boiling water and after 4 minutes remove the rosemary. The highly fragrant tisane can be drunk hot or cold.

lemon verbena

Take a flowering spray of lemon verbena (leaves intact) and place in a cup. Add boiling water and infuse for 4 minutes. Remove the flowers and foliage and enjoy a warm, lemon-flavoured drink that is pale golden in colour and wonderfully refreshing. Add honey for flavour and sweetness, or drink it chilled.

lavender

Place three sprigs of lavender flowers in a cup. Pour over boiling water and leave to infuse for 4 minutes before removing the flowers. The tisane will be pale blue with an uplifting lavender scent.

bergamot

The Oswegan Indians of North America made tea from bergamot leaves. After the Boston Tea Party in 1773 colonial settlers adopted the practice as a tea substitute. The flowers taste like the leaves but are sweeter and more flamboyant. To prepare, pour hot water on to a head of bergamot mixed with 2.5ml/ ½tsp of orange pekoe tea. Allow to infuse, then strain and drink.

chamomile

Chamomile flowers make one of the best known sedative teas, which, like lime blossom, is meant to induce a gentle sleep. Use three or four flower-heads only and add a little honey if you wish. The fragrance of chamomile tisane is powerful and attractive.

lime blossom

Use five or six fresh lime flowers for each cup and add hot, but not boiling, water. Steep for no longer than 3–4 minutes, then strain. Drink hot or cold, with lemon or sweetened with honey. It is a pale lemon colour and tastes surprisingly creamy.

peppermint

Just one sprig of leaves and flowers is enough to flavour a delicious tisane that has a very strong peppermint flavour without being overpowering. Served hot or cold, this is definitely a tisane to treat yourself with when you are feeling in need of refreshment.

cold drinks, punches
and cordials

sparkling elderflower drink

Elderflowers have a heady, musky scent and it is this fragrance that has made elderflower such a popular ingredient for drinks. Choose only really fresh flowers, just as they are beginning to open, when their flavour is at its best. Shake off any insects before use.

Makes 4.5 litres/1 gallon

600G/1¼LB SUGAR

4.5L/1 GALLON WATER

6–8 LARGE HEADS OF YOUNG ELDERFLOWERS, DRY AND
     FREE FROM INSECTS

2 LEMONS, SLICED

30ML/2TBSP WHITE WINE VINEGAR

1 Dissolve the sugar in 2.25l/4pts hot (not boiling) water. Add a further 2.25l/4pts of cold water.

2 When cool add the elderflowers, the sliced lemons and white wine vinegar.

3 Leave to stand for 24–48 hours, then strain into strong glass bottles and cork tightly. (It might be safer to use wires to hold down the tops.) The drink will be ready to serve in about 6 days.

summer punch

Summertime means a long, cool drink and a lazy afternoon. The beautiful borage flowers add the final essential ingredient. Here, the tastes of cucumber and mint are complemented by the flavour of the borage flower.

Serves 4–6

SEVERAL SPRIGS OF BORAGE

¼ CUCUMBER

1 SMALL ORANGE

¼ BOTTLE PIMM'S, CHILLED

SEVERAL SPRIGS OF MINT

ICE CUBES

1 BOTTLE LEMONADE (LEMON SODA), GINGER BEER OR GINGER ALE

1 To prepare the flowers, remove each flower-head from the green calyx by gently teasing it out. It should come away easily.

2 Halve the cucumber lengthways, then cut into thin slices. Chop the orange into small chunks, leaving the skin on. Put in a large jug and add the Pimm's and mint, followed by the borage flowers and ice cubes.

3 Pour in the lemonade (lemon soda), ginger beer or ginger ale, and stir gently to mix. Serve in tall glasses with extra flowers on top of each glass.

preserving flowers

Flowers can be preserved for use in the kitchen in many varied and glorious ways – as colourful butters, scented oils, aromatic vinegars and delicious sugars. With the addition of egg white and sugar, they are transformed into crystallized flowers that will grace any cake, cookie, mousse or roulade.

floral butters

Floral butters are a delightful and easy way of preserving flowers for use in the kitchen. They will keep for 2 weeks or more in an air-tight container in the fridge, and in the freezer they can be kept for up to 3 months. Floral butters look and taste good, and are extremely versatile.

Savoury butters can be spread on crusty bread, open sandwiches, bagels, rolls, or crackers. Try chive-flower butter with egg toppings, dill-flower butter with salmon, or sage-flower butter with pâtés or frankfurters. They can also be served with fresh vegetables. Try mint-flower butter with fresh new potatoes, or thyme-flower butter with steamed baby carrots.

Sweet floral butters are just as delicious, but their uses are different. A handful of scented fresh rose petals mixed with butter and icing (confectioner's) sugar will transform a plain layer cake into something memorable. You don't have to use only one kind of flower – try a combination of violets and primroses to make butter icing (frosting) for a Mother's Day cake.

floral oils

Flowers have a short season of availability and need to be preserved if they are to be enjoyed once the season has passed. One of the best ways to preserve their flavour is to make floral oils. The flowers are steeped in the oil for a week before being discarded, but the flavour lingers on and floral oils will last for up to 3 months, which gives you the chance to savour some unique flavours long after the flowers have disappeared. Floral oils are a very easy way of making the most of a bumper crop of summer flowers such as marjoram or lavender.

For sweeter flowers such as lavender, cowslips, or rose petals it is probably best to use a light sunflower oil. For the hearty flavours of hyssop, fennel, dill, mint, marjoram, thyme and basil use olive oil, or you might like to try walnut or even hazelnut oil. The results will be very different but well worth the experiment.

Many of the floral oils can be used to enhance particular kinds of dishes – lavender or hyssop oil may be used to sear chicken before cooking it in a casserole. Fennel or dill oil could be used to fry fish; sage oil might be used to baste pork or turkey. Marjoram or lavender oil both work well drizzled over a pizza just before it goes in the oven. Try thyme oil with

tomatoes or mushrooms before roasting. Or use thyme, pot marigold or marjoram oil as a dressing for pasta. Mint, salad rocket (arugula) or violet oil would all make wonderful additions to a vinaigrette, and will all result in remarkably different flavours. It is also possible to make oil from roses and rosemary flowers. The list of flavours is almost endless.

floral butter balls

Makes 50g/2oz

30ML/2TBSP FLOWERS;
THYME FLOWERS WERE
USED HERE

50G/2OZ UNSALTED
BUTTER, SOFTENED

1 Remove the individual
thyme florets or flowers
from the flower-head and
mix with softened butter.

This technique can be used with any of the savoury flowers. Where large petals are used, such as pot marigolds, you may prefer to snip them smaller.

2 Use wooden butter
boards or spoons to
make balls. Refrigerate
until ready to use.

3 Place thyme butter balls
on top of the vegetables.

mixed-flower butter dish

Makes 115g/4oz

60ML/4TBSP FLOWERS;
SAGE AND CHIVES WERE
USED HERE

115G/4OZ UNSALTED
BUTTER

1 Place a layer of chive
and sage flowers in
the middle of a dish. Place
half the butter over the
flowers. Sprinkle more
of the flowers on top.

Here, sage and chive flowers are combined to form layers of flowers between unsalted butter but you can use any of the flowers suggested opposite. Left for 24 hours, the flavour of the flowers impregnates the butter and creates a visual centrepiece for the table.

2 Add the second half
of butter and press
down gently to create a
good seal. Press additional
flowers around the four
sides of the butter.

3 Scatter more flowers
over the top of the
butter if you wish. Cover
and refrigerate for
24 hours before use.
Use to butter scones.

marjoram-flower oil

This wonderfully fragrant oil is very simple to make and can be used in so many different ways. Mix it with breadcrumbs and garlic to top baked mushrooms, tomatoes or peppers, or use it to cook an aromatic omelette.

Makes 450ml/¾pt/scant 2 cups

30–40 MARJORAM FLOWER CLUSTERS, CLEAN, DRY AND
FREE OF INSECTS

450ML/¾PT/SCANT 2 CUPS OLIVE OIL (NOT EXTRA VIRGIN)

1 Fill a jam jar with lots of marjoram flower-heads. It is not necessary to remove the flowers individually – a few leaves will not matter.

2 Cover completely with the olive oil. It is important that the oil covers the flowers – any that are not covered will go mouldy. Place the jar on a sunny windowsill for 1 week. Shake the jar from time to time.

3 Carefully strain the flower oil into a jug (pitcher) through a piece of muslin (cheesecloth), or alternatively through a clean coffee filter.

4 Pour the strained liquid into a pretty bottle. Once strained, the oil will keep for up to 3 months.

floral vinegars

Floral vinegars make a delicious alternative to ordinary cider or white wine vinegar in a vinaigrette. Violet vinegar is made by placing petals from scented blue violets in white wine vinegar for about 4 weeks. Use a screw-top jar and fill to the top with violets and vinegar. Screw the top securely and then place on a sunny windowsill. The sun helps release all the oils from the flowers. Shake occasionally and, when the liquid turns blue, strain and use as required.

Mix up a vinaigrette to serve with the violet and primrose salad, or try it with seafood salads or grilled vegetables. Parma violets also make an excellent vinaigrette; either purple or pink, they are now easily available in spring. Fortunately, violets flower over a period of several weeks so it is possible to make more than one batch.

mint-flower vinegar

This makes an excellent vinegar for salad dressings, and can be used in a classic vinaigrette dressing. The mint flavour will be particularly appreciated in winter when the fresh leaves are unavailable.

Makes 450ml/¾pt/2 cups

120ML/8TBSP MINT FLOWERS WITH STEMS
   AND LEAVES ATTACHED
450ML/¾PT/2 CUPS WHITE WINE VINEGAR

1 Place the mint flowers in a jar with a non-metallic lid. A kilner jar is ideal.

2 Heat the vinegar gently in a glass or steel saucepan, but do not allow it to boil.

3 Pour the heated vinegar over the flowers, bringing the level to within 1.5cm/½in of the rim of the jar.

4 Allow the mixture to cool before putting the lid on.

5 Leave for 3–4 weeks, then strain and pour into a clean jar or a recycled vinegar bottle.

6 Add a few fresh mint flowers (on their stems) for decoration and label the jar or bottle.

floral sugars

This is an easy but effective way of capturing the flavour of sweet flowers. Many different types can be made, including violet, pink, citrus flower, rose, lavender and mint. The stronger the scent, the more tasty the results.

Makes 225g/8oz/2 cups

225G/8OZ/2 CUPS ICING (CONFECTIONER'S), CASTER
   (SUPERFINE) OR GRANULATED SUGAR
90–180ML/6–12TBSP WHOLE OR CHOPPED
   FLOWER PETALS

1 Place the sugar and petals into a food processor and blend. Store in a sealed container for 1 week.

2 Sift the sugar to remove the flower petals and put the sugar into a jar or another airtight container. Use it to make butter-cream fillings for cakes, and to add flavour to meringues and sorbets.

crystallized flowers

Crystallizing flower petals is a simple and very effective way of preserving them for future use, and the sugar enhances their delicate flavour. Use individually or try different combinations to create a masterpiece.

I EGG WHITE

50G/2OZ CASTER (SUPERFINE) SUGAR

LOTS OF INDIVIDUAL PETALS AND/OR ENTIRE FLOWERS

1 A simple way to crystallize flowers is to use egg white and caster (superfine) sugar, but they will only last up to 2 days. First gather your flowers when they are dry. Take each petal individually or the flower as a whole, depending on the effect you want to achieve. Place the egg white and sugar in separate saucers.

2 To crystallize petals, take each individual petal or whole flower-head and paint the petals both front and back with the egg white.

3 Lightly cover both sides with caster sugar. You will find that it sticks to the damp surface.

4 Lay individual petals, evenly spaced, on a sheet of baking parchment and keep them in a warm, dry place overnight, or until crisp. Store the petals in an air-tight container until needed, for up to 2 days.

5 After treating whole flower-heads, attach a piece of thread to the base of the flower or push florist's wire through the base. Drape the heads around a glass by attaching the thread with tape or bending the wires.

frozen flowers

Nothing could be more attractive than preserving flowers in ice. You can use floral ice cubes to cool your summer drinks or as the centrepiece in a chilled soup. The process for making the ice cubes is simple, but first you must judge the shape and size of the individual flowers you want to freeze compared with the size of the compartments of the ice tray.

Makes 2 trays of ice cubes

A SELECTION OF FRESH, CLEAN FLOWERS

WATER TO FILL 2 ICE TRAYS

1 First prepare the flowers. Snip the florets off some scented geraniums. Remove as much of the stem and green parts as possible. You may get as many as four or six florets from one flower-head. Use the florets individually or as little groups.

2 Pour water in the ice-cube tray, filling it about half full. (You don't have to use water – you can use lemonade or fruit juice. The contrast of fruit and flower will add a delicious flavour to your drink as the ice melts.)

3 Place the florets or individual petals on top of the water, using tweezers if preferred. Put in the freezer and allow to freeze until solid.

4 Remove from the freezer and add more water to bring the level up to the top of the ice-cube tray. Leave in the freezer until needed.